Published by Ladybird Books Ltd
A Penguin Company
Penguin Books Ltd, 80 Strand, London WC2R 0RL, UK
Penguin Books Australia Ltd, Camberwell, Victoria, Australia
Penguin Books (NZ) Ltd, Cnr Airbourne and Rosedale Roads, Albany, Auckland, 1310, New Zealand

3 5 7 9 10 8 6 4 2

© LADYBIRD BOOKS MMV

Printed in Italy

Inventors

written by Lorraine Horsley
illustrated by John Dillow,
Martin Sanders and Chris Rothero

Ladybird

Inventors and their inventions

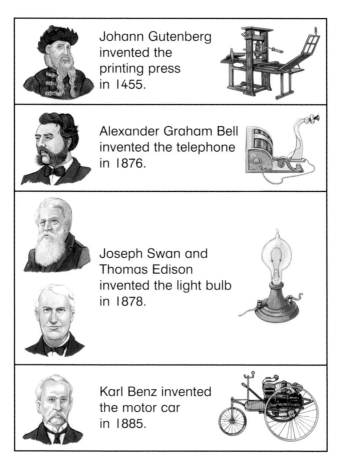

Johann Gutenberg invented the printing press in 1455.

Alexander Graham Bell invented the telephone in 1876.

Joseph Swan and Thomas Edison invented the light bulb in 1878.

Karl Benz invented the motor car in 1885.

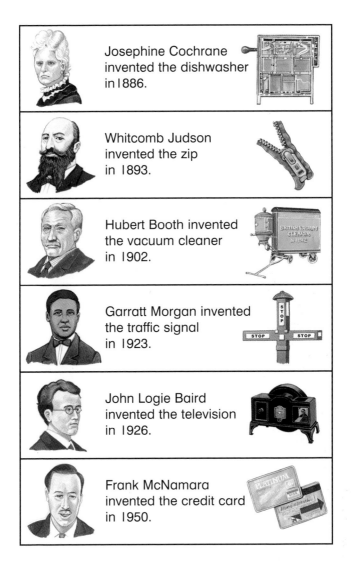

Josephine Cochrane invented the dishwasher in 1886.

Whitcomb Judson invented the zip in 1893.

Hubert Booth invented the vacuum cleaner in 1902.

Garratt Morgan invented the traffic signal in 1923.

John Logie Baird invented the television in 1926.

Frank McNamara invented the credit card in 1950.

Before vacuum cleaners were invented, people had to clean their houses with brushes and dustpans.

The first traffic signals had stop and go written on them. Today, traffic signals use lights.

Before telephones were invented, people could not talk to each other if they were not in the same place. They had to write letters.

The first credit cards could not be used in many places. Today, credit cards can be used to pay for things everywhere.

Can you match the inventor to the invention?

Johann
Gutenberg

Alexander
Graham Bell

Joseph
Swan

Thomas
Edison

Karl
Benz

Josephine
Cochrane

Whitcomb
Judson

Hubert
Booth

Garratt
Morgan

John Logie
Baird

Frank
McNamara

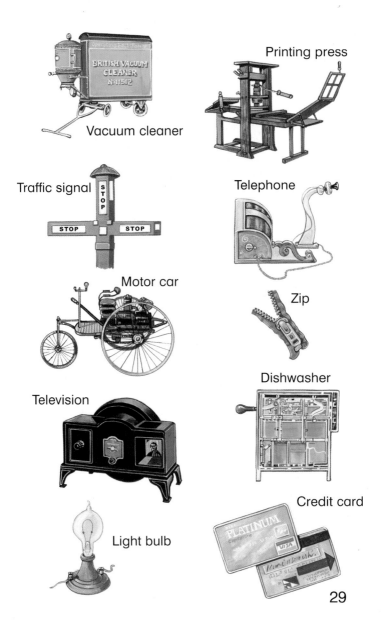

Vacuum cleaner

Printing press

Traffic signal

Telephone

Motor car

Zip

Television

Dishwasher

Light bulb

Credit card

29

Index